Buffalo Sunrise

The Story of a North American Giant

Diane Swanson

Whitecap Books

Vancouver / Toronto

Edited by Elaine Jones
Cover design by Warren Clark
Interior design by Margaret Ng
Typeset by Margaret Ng
Cover photograph by Jeff Foott

Printed and bound in Hong Kong.

Canadian Cataloguing in Publication Data

Swanson, Diane, 1944–
    Buffalo Sunrise

    Includes index.
    ISBN 1-55110-378-8

    1. Bison, American—Juvenile literature. I. Title.
QL737.U53S92 1995   j599.73'58   C95-910855-6

Acknowledgments

My sincerest thanks to Hal Reynolds of the Canadian Wildlife Service, Eleanor Verbicky-Todd, an independent research consultant, Ruth McConnell of the Provincial Museum of Alberta, and Shirley Bruised Head of Head-Smashed-In Buffalo Jump, who each reviewed sections of this book and provided valuable comments; David Poll of Parks Canada, who contributed very useful advice and information; Lorna Perry of Lethbridge and Dorothy MacMillan of Calgary, who kindly supported and encouraged my research in Alberta; and Wayne Swanson, who, as always, helped me in innumerable ways.

Contents

One buffalo can trigger a stampede of hundreds—a spectacular sight.

Let's Hear It for the Buffalo!

A magnificent beast is the buffalo—strong, speedy, and nimble. And of all the land animals in North America, it is, by far, the biggest.

Millions upon millions of buffaloes once roamed this continent. At times, they moved in masses so huge they shook the plains.

The native people who shared these plains depended on the buffalo for food, shelter, clothing, and more. Later, pioneers from Europe also hunted the buffalo for meat and other goods.

But overhunting quickly drove this incredible animal to near extinction. By 1890, it had almost disappeared.

For more than 100 years, North Americans have worked to help the buffalo survive. To make sure it lives on as a free and wild creature, there's still more work ahead.

So the story of the North American buffalo is a story of the past, the present, and the future. It's a story about the importance of sharing our world with wildlife. It's a story to celebrate another sunrise for the buffalo.

Its thick, woolly winter coat helps the buffalo survive cold winters.

Woolly Giant

More than 400 years ago, Spanish explorers in North America spotted a shaggy, brown beast they had never seen before. They said it had horns like a cow, a mane like a lion, and a hump like a camel. And when it ran, it held its tail like a scorpion—straight up.

This awesome beast was the buffalo, a giant in the cow family. Its size alone was enough to amaze early explorers. It amazes people even today. In fact, the buffalo is the biggest land animal in both Canada and the United States. A male can weigh 2200 pounds (a tonne) and stand as tall as a doorway—more than 6½ feet (2 metres).

There is only one kind, or species, of buffalo in North America, but within that there are two groups: the wood buffalo and the plains buffalo. Wood buffaloes are generally bigger, darker, and woollier, and they live mostly in wooded parts of northern Canada. Plains buffaloes live on grasslands in both Canada and the United States.

Spaniard Francisco Lopez de Gomara published this drawing of a North American buffalo in the early 1550s. At that time, many explorers thought the buffalo looked as if it were part cow, part camel, and part lion.

Some people, including scientists, correctly call North American buffaloes *bison*. When they talk of *buffaloes*, they are referring to related animals that live in Asia and Africa. But for hundreds of years, most people in the United States and Canada have used the word *buffalo* for the North American animal.

An Awesome Animal

As big and heavy as the buffalo is, it's anything but clumsy. It can pick its way along rocky ledges, walking where no horse can. The wood buffalo has climbed high up tall mountains—even beyond levels where trees are able to grow.

4

It's easy for a buffalo to travel over rocky or uneven land because it moves on tiptoe. On each small foot, the tips of its two biggest toes are covered with a tough, hard coating. The buffalo does all its walking and running on these covered toes, which are called hooves. Its other two toes, called dewclaws, are so small they never touch the ground. Cows' feet are built the same way, but few kinds of cows climb like buffaloes do.

Despite its great weight, the buffalo can walk quickly and can run as fast as 35 miles (55 kilometres) an hour. A racehorse can run faster but only for about a sixth of a mile (a quarter of a kilometre). The buffalo can run fast for nearly four times that distance.

It can even walk fast in snow, unless the snow is very deep. Using its bulky body like a plow, the buffalo pushes its way through. Its hooves pack the snow down hard, making an easy path for others to follow.

The buffalo is also a strong swimmer, able to battle powerful currents to cross rivers. But sometimes it seems to swim just because it wants to. It may paddle into a lake only to turn around and paddle back again. And it may choose to swim across a pond even though it's easier to walk around the water.

Harsh winters can be hard on the buffalo, but it's able to survive better than many animals. As the weather turns cool, it grows thicker skin, more fat, and a longer, denser wool coat. It finds grass to eat by sweeping away shallow snow with its beard. Sometimes it burrows through deeper snow, pushing with its nose or swinging its huge head and

Oversize Buffalo

A million years ago, the North American buffalo was even bigger than it is now. Tip to tip, its ever-growing horns spread more than 6 1/2 feet (2 metres). That's over three times the spread of horns on today's buffalo.

This massive animal shared its world with other furry giants, such as the bulky short-faced bear and the elephant-like mammoth, which stood over 10 feet (3 metres) tall. The buffalo held its own in this oversize world, but through the years it gradually became smaller. So did its horns.

Scientists think that having shorter horns made it easier for buffaloes to live together. Without such wide-spreading headgear, they were less dangerous to one another.

Even in water, buffaloes stay together, swimming across rivers as wide as half a mile (nearly a kilometre).

neck. It can work its way through more than 3 feet (a metre) of snow to reach food.

And what an eater it is! A long, thick tongue presses grass against its lips or stuffs the grass into its mouth. Then its bottom teeth slice it off. After very little chewing, the buffalo swallows the grass, sending it to the first part of a big, four-part stomach. There the grass softens while the buffalo eats more.

Hours later, when the buffalo is safe and contented, it brings the swallowed food back to its mouth. Standing or lying down, it chews its *cud*— the returned food—a wad at a time. The buffalo chews and chews. Then it swallows the rechewed food, which passes through all parts of its stomach. This system of chewing and digesting makes it possible for buffaloes to live well on tough grass.

All Together Now

Buffaloes are very sociable animals. They sleep together, eat together, and travel together. Bad weather and danger often draw them especially close.

Sometimes they form herds of several hundred. But much of the time, the females—called cows—and their calves live in close groups of about 20; the males—called bulls—

Buffalo Birds

*H*erds of buffaloes attract birds. Magpies, starlings, blackbirds, and cowbirds know that a buffalo stirs up a lot to eat. Its hooves disturb insects, such as grasshoppers, that live among the grasses. Then the birds swoop down and snatch up the insects.

Sometimes, cowbirds—the most common buffalo birds— hop along a buffalo's back and feed on the flies that often hover there. The birds can eat nonstop for as long as half an hour before flying off.

Buffalo birds help the buffaloes by eating some of the insects that annoy them. But the birds also gain much by hanging around the herds. Not only do they find a supply of insects, they use the buffaloes as a place to rest. That's especially helpful in places where few trees grow. And in cold weather, the birds can warm their feet in a woolly buffalo coat.

Butting heads over a cow, these bulls lock horns in a dust-stirring battle of strength.

usually form more scattered groups of up to 5. At breeding times, these groups all gather together.

Not all buffaloes are equal. Usually, the bigger and heavier the animal, the more important it is in the herd. Among buffaloes of the same size, age, strength, and fighting skills help decide who is more important. Bulls usually rank higher than cows, and cows rank higher than calves.

By ranking themselves from most to least important, buffaloes live more peaceably. They don't fight over scarce food or water; instead, the most important buffalo takes what it needs, then the next most important moves in, and so on. Even a spot in the shade, if there isn't much around, goes first to the top-ranking buffalo.

At mating times, bulls sometimes fight over cows. Two bulls may charge each other at top speed, butting heads, shoving, and pushing until the weaker one moves off. But more often, one bull tries to drive the other away by swinging his horns, snorting, and making other loud noises.

He may also scrape the ground with his front hoof, roll on the ground, or charge a tree, jabbing his horns into the trunk. Occasionally, he may even uproot a young tree. All this action warns the other bull to leave—or else.

Rubbing against a tree in spring helps the buffalo shed its heavy winter coat.

9

The hump on a wood buffalo, like this one, is squarish. A plains buffalo has a rounded hump.

Buffalo Banter

Because buffaloes live together, it's not surprising that they talk. Their "words" are grunts, snorts, and bellows. They even make squeaky noises by grinding their teeth together.

As they travel in herds, noisemaking helps buffaloes—especially the cows and calves—keep track of each other. To call her calf, a cow may grunt softly and slowly. If the calf wants help—or just attention—it makes its own strained little grunts.

Some grunts are warnings to other animals or people to stay away. A bull also gives warnings by snorting and stamping its feet. And it bellows: with mouth hanging open, tongue dangling, and belly heaving, it roars like a lion. Bellows are especially loud at mating times, when bulls try to keep other bulls away from their cows.

If one bull hears another bull bellow back, the first bull bellows louder than before. Bulls sometimes bellow back at clouds that "bellow" with thunder. The loudest noise a bull makes can be heard at least 3 miles (5 kilometres) away.

When some bulls start bellowing, they don't seem to want to stop. They roar while they run. They roar while they swim. They even roar while they eat. Their food often falls out when they bellow with their mouths full, but they don't seem to mind. They're often more interested in making noise than in eating.

The buffalo also uses body language. It makes threats by staring, lowering its head, or pawing the ground. And it says several things with

Buffalo Sense

*P*eople watch for danger, but buffaloes smell it. If a grizzly bear is lurking nearby, the buffaloes might spot it when it moves, but they will likely detect it first with their noses.

Their ears are very sensitive, too. If the bear snaps a twig—even 500 feet (150 metres) away—the buffaloes will hear it. Their sense of hearing also allows them to pick out different tones and rhythms in the sounds other buffaloes make.

When they rub against rough tree trunks and boulders, buffaloes use their sense of touch. Often they return to the same boulders—called "rubbing stones"—time after time, gradually wearing them down. Besides feeling good, the rubbing helps buffaloes groom their fur and skin.

All that rubbing has sometimes caused problems for people. Buffaloes have knocked down poles and even old cabins by rubbing their heavy bodies against them. To try to keep buffaloes away, people in the 1800s put sharp metal spikes on telegraph poles. But when the animals scratched themselves on these spikes, it felt so good they rubbed against the poles even more.

Artists don't always draw animals the way they really look. The plains buffalo in this 1844 painting has an unusual head, but its tail is quite realistic— curved and raised as a warning sign.

its tail. A swishing tail lets others know that the buffalo is happy or excited. For instance, a calf swishes its tail when it drinks its mother's milk or plays with another calf. A tail sticking up usually means the buffalo is worried. Buffaloes often raise their tails when they check out something they haven't seen before. And rival bulls in mating season usually meet with their tails up. If those tails are S-shaped, the bulls are really angry.

However, when a tail is whipping madly about, the buffalo may be saying nothing at all. It may just be swatting flies.

Chapter 2

Great Provider

It's hard to imagine an animal more important to anyone than the buffalo was to the native people of North America. For thousands of years, it provided food, clothing, and shelter to many native nations, including the Arikara, Arapaho, Assiniboine, Blackfoot Confederacy, Cheyenne, Comanche, Cree, Crow, Gros Ventre, Hidatsa, Kiowa, Kiowa-Apache, Mandan, Pawnee, Ponca, Sarcee, and Teton-Dakota.

Native North Americans valued and respected the spirit of the buffalo as well as its body. The animal played an important role in many of their celebrations, ceremonies, stories, dances, and songs. Much of this chapter describes what the buffalo meant to Blackfoot families living on the Alberta-Montana plains around 1870.

As this nineteenth-century art shows, a young calf normally stays close to its mother.

Close Contact

Even as children, the Blackfoot watched the buffalo and learned its ways well. That helped them become skilled and respectful hunters—and it was also just plain fun.

During buffalo chases, young calves sometimes lost their mothers and followed the hunters' horses back to camp. Some of these calves might be only a few weeks old. Others

Peeking around its mother, this calf stopped playing long enough to check out the photographer taking its picture.

might be a couple of months—just old enough to start developing humps on their backs.

Typically, the calves would graze and rest when they first reached a camp, then head to a nearby river for a drink. Often they would start playing at the river, racing along the bank and leaping in and out of the water.

Calf play delighted the Blackfoot children. Sometimes they would try to join in a race with the calves. But the young buffaloes in a camp tended to switch games quickly. They might stop racing along a river bank and start dashing back and forth across the grass. Or they might gallop in circles around a group of children, grunting, snorting, and sneezing as they ran.

Almost as suddenly as the calves started to play, they stopped. Panting like dogs, they would flop down on the grass to rest. It might be hours before they would rise again.

Then one calf might start prancing about and butt a resting calf. If it got no response, it might turn to a tree, charge a low branch, or kick the trunk. Common calf antics such as these often made the children laugh.

White Jewel

*I*n August 1994, on a Wisconsin farm, a white calf was born to a brown buffalo. So rare was this calf that her owners named her Miracle. Hundreds of thousands of people watched her on their TV screens and read about her in their newspapers. Others traveled from across the continent to see her for themselves. Some brought her gifts of sweet grass and small, round nets called dream-catchers.

A buffalo has about one chance in 10 million of being born white. For centuries, many native North American people believed that the white buffalo was sacred. Some thought its snowy hide had the power to cure illnesses or to keep warriors safe in battle. Some believed that a woman who had once saved a tribe from starving had turned into a white buffalo; her return would signal great change.

When Miracle arrived, one of the Aani people told news reporters, "Everything is reborn: thought, hope, life, all of these things."

Good Use

In the Blackfoot camp, the days that followed a buffalo hunt buzzed with activity. Everyone was busy. There was meat to process, hides to clean, and things to make.

People scurried about preparing big piles of buffalo meat. They boiled some, roasted some, and dried some. And they made a nutritious food, called pemmican, by heating dried meat, breaking it up, and pounding it fine.

Then they added melted buffalo fat and, sometimes, dried berries. Using a long stick, they packed the mixture tightly into rawhide sacks. Then they jumped on the sacks to make them more solid. Each sack held about 100 pounds (45 kilograms) of the mixture, which kept for up to 30 years—less if it contained berries. Families ate the pemmican just as it was. Occasionally, they stewed some in water.

Preparing buffalo hides also meant a lot of work. The Blackfoot wet them and stretched them across the ground, staking them in place. Then they scraped off the flesh with a bone tool called a flesher and dried the hides in the sun. Depending on how they wanted to use the hides, they scraped the hair off some of them.

Buffalo hides covering wooden poles formed cone-shaped tents, called tipis, in this Blackfoot camp.

The people used these stiff hides, called rawhides, to make things such as drums, rattles, and carrying cases. Hides used for clothing, bedding, and tipi covers needed more work to soften them. So the Blackfoot made up a mixture of fat, brains, and liver from the buffalo and worked it into some of the rawhides. Then they soaked the hides in water and stretched them again. They also smoked some of the hides so that they would shed water more easily.

The children in the Blackfoot camp kept busy, too. They helped make rattles by stringing buffalo hooves on cords cut from rawhide. And they packed buffalo hair into hide saddles. Some of the hair was set aside to twist into ropes for belts and bridles, but there was a bit left to stuff into dolls and balls for playing with later. The children knew that other toys would come from the buffalo, too—such as spinning tops from horns. And when winter came, they could race down snowy hills on rawhide toboggans and sleds with runners made of buffalo ribs.

Genuine Respect

Blackfoot tribes held many celebrations and ceremonies to honor the buffalo and to draw on the powers they believed it had. Of all the animals they respected, the buffalo ranked among the highest. It was a symbol of food and shelter; it was sacred.

Families always celebrated successful buffalo hunts. Late into the night, they gathered around fires, feasting, singing, laughing, and dancing. And as they did on many evenings all year round, they told stories—especially about the buffalo. Some tales explained how the buffalo came to be and described its great strength and supernatural powers. Others told of the deeds of hunters, including a camp of ghosts who chased buffaloes.

In many Blackfoot ceremonies, the buffalo appeared in the songs, dances, and prayers. And the people often used different parts of the animal for their special dress. Some wore the scalp and horns of the buffalo as a bonnet; others wore headdresses made from woolly hides. Some covered themselves with heavy buffalo robes; others wore belts decorated with dangling buffalo tails.

The people of many native North American nations made bull boats by stretching buffalo hides over boughs. The boats were strong enough to carry a horse.

All in One

Besides food, the Blackfoot had more than 100 uses for
the parts of the buffalo. Here are a few of them.

Hides

Tipi covers
Bedding
Clothing
Shields
Sheaths
Saddles
Bags and pouches
Ropes, tie strings
Water troughs
Horseshoes
Toboggans
Masks
Headdresses
Balls
Dolls

Sinew (tissue joining muscle and bone)
Thread
Bow strings

Horns

Arrow points
Masks
Headdress ornaments
Powder flasks
Spoons
Cups

Hooves

Glue
Rattles

Tails

Ornaments
Fly swatters

Bones

Scraping tools
Paint brushes
Sled runners
Dice

Organs

Buckets, basins
Glue
Hide softener

Fat

Hide softener
Pipe polish

Hair

Ornaments
Stuffing

Each summer, the Blackfoot feasted on buffalo tongues in one of their most important ceremonies—the Sun Dance. They built a frame for a dance lodge, using poles tied with strips cut from the hide of a buffalo—one that hunters killed specially for the event.

The Blackfoot who took part in the Sun Dance first cleansed themselves by sweating in the hot, moist air of a special lodge called a sweat lodge. It was made of willows covered with buffalo robes. On top of the lodge—or next to it—they placed a painted buffalo skull stuffed with grass.

From the center of the Sun Dance lodge hung a buffalo tail. Below it lay a fire pit. Blackfoot warriors stood beneath the tail and recited stories of all their brave deeds. For each deed they described, they placed one stick on the fire. The greater the warrior, the higher the fire. The one who was the greatest of all was the one who told enough stories to scorch the buffalo tail.

Buffalo Calling

*F*or many years, the Blackfoot performed a drama to help bring the buffalo close. Elderly men pulled on head-dresses and buffalo robes and lay near the water, like buf-faloes. One young man would "frighten" them by throwing a stone and burning dried buffalo dung, which he floated on the water. Then he would jump on his horse, shouting loudly as he rode close to the "buffaloes."

After he roused them all to their feet, the young man herded them to camp. There they sang and they danced, moving the way buffaloes moved. The herder told stories of his adventure to all the people who gathered at the camp.

As part of their Sun Dance ceremonies, the Blackfoot set out a painted
buffalo skull stuffed with grass. Yellow represents the sun;
black, the night; and brown, the day.

Chapter 3

Mighty Prey

Hunting a huge, fast-running beast like the buffalo was no easy job. It was especially hard when hunters traveled by foot and used crude weapons. Yet for thousands of years, people in North America managed to hunt great herds of buffaloes all year round.

The wandering ways of buffaloes often made them hard to find. Between late spring and early fall, people tried to trail them across the plains, moving from one grazing ground to another. In colder seasons, some people followed northern herds into woods, river valleys, and other sheltered spots.

Sometimes the hunters worked alone or in small groups. At other times, they formed large parties to catch the number of buffaloes they needed. Their methods ranged from simple shooting to complex trapping, but they all required courage.

Driving and Trapping

Many bands in North America hunted buffaloes by driving them over tall, steep cliffs, called buffalo jumps. One of the biggest and oldest jumps is Head-Smashed-In Buffalo Jump in the Province of Alberta. As long as 5,700 years ago, people used this jump to drive herds off a stone cliff 60 feet (18 metres) high, and countless people have used it since.

The job may sound simple, but the grasslands where the buffaloes grazed were up to 9 miles (14.5 kilometres) away. Driving the herds through hilly country all the way to the cliff wasn't easy. That's why people set up "drive lanes" to move the buffaloes in the right direction. They formed the lanes by piling up rocks every 15 to 30 feet (4.5 to 9 metres). Then they heaped the piles high with dirt, brush, and buffalo chips—dried dung.

Getting the animals to move toward the drive lanes was the work of strong, young athletes called buffalo runners. Carefully chosen and trained, they could run fast and far. They understood the buffalo and knew its ways well. They had patience and courage.

The Legend of Head-Smashed-In

A long time ago, the People of the Plains were driving a great herd of buffaloes toward a stony cliff. But one young man decided to wait at the bottom of the cliff. He wanted to watch the buffaloes as they tumbled over. For protection, he stood beneath a rocky ledge and pressed himself against the cliff.

That day, the hunt was very successful; many buffaloes fell. Bodies piled on bodies, and soon the young man found himself trapped—wedged between the buffaloes and the cliff.

When the hunt ended, the people gathered at the bottom of the cliff. There, among the animals, they found the body of the young man. The weight of the buffaloes had crushed his head. And from then on, the People of the Plains called that place Head-Smashed-In.

For centuries, native North Americans drove great buffalo herds over cliffs.
They hunted first on foot and, much later, on horseback.

Using rawhide snowshoes, hunters herded buffaloes into deep snowdrifts.
There they could shoot the trapped animals more easily.

Buffalo runners often wore hides of buffaloes or other animals, such as wolves and coyotes. They moved in close to a herd, careful to go only where the wind wouldn't carry their smell and warn the buffaloes. Gradually, they directed the animals toward the drive lanes by slapping hides on the ground, lighting small fires, calling like owls, or shouting.

As the herd neared a lane, a runner often tried to lure the buffaloes. Wearing a buffalo hide, he might bellow like a bull or imitate a calf to draw the herd forward. Disguised as a coyote or wolf, he might chase a calf along a lane so older buffaloes would move in to protect it.

Once the herd was inside a drive lane, other hunters— and, often, women and children—jumped up from behind the piles that lined the lane. They scared the animals by waving buffalo robes and shouting. Still more people moved in behind the herd as the frightened buffaloes sped closer and closer to the cliff.

As the buffaloes neared the steep cliff, the first dozen or so could see the sudden drop, but by then it was too late. Even if they could stop in time, the massive weight of the herd following close behind would push them over.

Many buffaloes died from the fall; others were injured or stunned. But the survivors didn't last long. With spears, arrows, and stone hammers, the band moved in and killed them all.

Buffalo runners and hunters didn't always drive buffaloes over cliffs. Sometimes they ran herds into swampy land or deep snowdrifts where the animals became trapped. Or they drove them down drive lanes to small canyons or

Buffalo Horse

Quivering with excitement, the horse brought its rider alongside a racing buffalo. The rider crouched forward and to the side, preparing to shoot. Then—whether or not the shot was made—the horse began to swerve away. It had to head for safety before the buffalo turned its horns against both horse and rider.

Hunters who used horses to chase buffaloes prized their buffalo horses. The success and safety of the hunt depended heavily on the horse. A good buffalo horse was fast and had the strength to run long distances. It could race across uneven ground without stumbling. It could get close to buffaloes but avoid their horns. It obeyed commands instantly, and it was brave.

Few horses had what it took to become buffalo horses. Hunters chose their animals carefully and trained them well, using patience and practice as their tools.

into corrals made of wood and brush draped with hides. The corrals weren't strong, but as long as they looked solid the buffaloes didn't try to break out, making them easy prey for the hunters.

Surrounding and Chasing

It would take a lot of courage to surround a buffalo herd. Yet native people in North America did just that—and on foot. Slowly, quietly, they formed a huge circle around grazing buffaloes. Then they edged forward, step by step, gradually making their circle smaller and tighter.

Days without wind were best for this kind of hunting. Then the buffaloes didn't smell danger until the people were close. But as soon as the herd picked up the scent, the buffaloes began to run. Whichever way they went, the people yelled and waved their robes. When the buffaloes turned and ran the other way, the same thing would happen. Soon they started to bunch together and run around in a circle. That's when the hunters moved closer and fired their arrows.

In the 1500s, the Spaniards brought horses to North America, and gradually native people started to ride. Sometimes they surrounded buffaloes on horseback as they had on foot. Sometimes they rode horses to drive herds over cliffs or into corrals. But when horses became common, hunters began killing buffaloes on the run.

*On foot or on horseback, hunters worked as a team to surround
buffalo herds, then moved in for the kill.*

Hunting buffaloes from trains was wasteful. Very seldom was a dead animal taken on board.

Using their swiftest horses, hunters approached a herd slowly. They hid among trees or boulders as they rode. When the time was right, their leader gave a signal—and the hunters charged. They each rode dangerously close alongside a buffalo before firing. Usually they preferred to shoot arrows, even after guns were introduced. From a speeding horse, arrows were easier to aim, and they marked the kills for the hunters.

In as little as 15 minutes, it was all over. Compared to other kinds of hunting—which often lasted several days—chasing buffaloes was very efficient.

Hunting on the Run and Hunting Still

As Europeans moved onto the North American plains, they, too, hunted buffaloes. In the early 1800s, pioneers often hunted in large groups. Mostly they used guns and chased buffaloes on horseback. They killed for food and hides, but many also enjoyed the chase.

Later, some Europeans came to hunt across North America just for fun. Among them was a rich Irish nobleman, St. George Gore, who traveled the plains with 40 servants, 70 horses, and wagons full of guns. His trip in the 1850s claimed 2,000 buffaloes.

Chasing buffaloes became a popular hobby among millionaires, who set up hunting parties for their friends. One party, in 1872, included royalty from Russia—Grand Duke Alexis. After firing wildly at a buffalo herd, he managed to shoot a large bull. Then he took the tail as a souvenir.

As hunting stories spread, excitement grew. Railroad companies, which had been laying track across the plains, offered people cheap trips to hunt buffaloes. As herds passed the trains, people inside opened their windows and fired their guns. Sometimes, the trains stopped and the passengers stepped out to shoot. But they left most of their prey to rot by the tracks.

Still, hunting for fun or food didn't kill as many buffaloes as hunting for hides. By the 1870s, people had discovered new ways of treating hides—and more uses for them. So hide hunters flocked to the plains, bringing better, faster-loading guns.

Rather than chasing buffaloes, these hunters often chose to *still hunt*—to shoot from one spot. They rode off to find a herd, then crept up to it by walking or even crawling. When

Winter Quest for Food

During a prairie winter around 1880, a missionary named John McDougall ran short of food for himself and his family. He formed a hunting party of six, and they set off to find buffaloes. A letter he wrote describes this hunt:

"The snow was about a foot [30 centimetres] deep on the level and, in the drifts, from two to four feet [up to about a metre] deep. The buffaloes, when they ran, made it fly in a thick cloud behind them. . . . Away jumped our eager horses and, shutting eyes and mouth, men and horses disappeared into the cloud. . . . Here were the prey right before us with their winter coats and every muscle stretched in flight. . . . I shot and secured three fat cows.

"The next day, it was much colder. We moved camp, made another hunt. . . . This time my horse fell twice with me; once my gun disappeared in a snowdrift, and I had quite a time finding it."

But John McDougall found his gun in time to hunt again. Soon he and the others had enough food to last well beyond the winter.

In this 1839 painting, a shot from a hunter brought down another buffalo.

they were less than 750 feet (230 metres) away, the hunters took cover and fired, shooting as many buffaloes as they could. Often the herd ran a short distance, and the hunters followed and fired again. But sometimes, the buffaloes stood their ground; they even seemed curious about the fallen animals. Then hunters were able to shoot many more.

Much of the hunters' success depended on their aim. If they struck the lungs, they brought down the buffaloes fast. But if they happened to hit a bull on his tough, thick forehead, their bullets usually bounced right off.

Hide hunters normally worked in teams of 4 to 12. These teams included the leader—who did the shooting—along with a helper who reloaded the rifles, a team of skinners who removed the hides from the buffaloes, and sometimes, a cook. A single hunter often killed 100 buffaloes a day, enough to keep the skinners busy from sunup to sundown.

Chapter 4

Helpful Ghost

Unlike the first Europeans on the North American plains, settlers of the late 1800s could only imagine the great herds that had once grazed there. These newcomers would never see thousands of buffaloes blanketing the plains, never feel the ground shaking as they ran, never hear the thundering of their hooves. Hunters had ended all that; very few buffaloes had escaped their fire.

But the great herds had left behind many gifts: trails to travel; bones, hooves, and horns to gather; and memories to warm the heart and stir the imagination. Much of this chapter describes what the buffalo meant to settlers living on the Alberta-Montana plains around 1890.

From 1883 to 1913, the only buffaloes many people saw appeared in the Wild West shows advertised in booklets such as this one.

Tracing the Trails

Traveling by horse and wagon on the plains, families were grateful to have a network of trails. Not only did the network help them find their way, the trails usually led to watering spots for their horses.

The buffaloes had created these trails by following the same routes year after year. As they moved across the prairie, huge herds wore deep paths in the ground. Trails they had used for hundreds of years gradually widened, forming prairie highways. Some settlers called them "bison streets."

Where herds had come together at places such as rivers, the trails were especially well marked. Heavy hooves had packed the earth hard—too hard for plants to grow back even long after buffaloes had stopped walking the trails.

The herds had created the most efficient routes from one place to another. Their trails often ran in straight lines, even when they passed through woody or hilly areas. And they led to points along rivers where crossings were easiest to make.

Because buffaloes were so nimble, they sometimes chose a route along a rocky ledge. The route was easy for them to use but too narrow and steep for wagons. Still, that wasn't

The Wild West of Buffalo Bill

Work crews laying train tracks across the United States lived on fresh buffalo meat. And the most famous hunter ever hired to supply this meat was a young man named William Frederick Cody. Starting in 1867 and working single-handedly, he shot thousands of buffaloes for the railway workers. They called him Buffalo Bill, a name that stuck for life. Even children chanted:

Buffalo Bill, Buffalo Bill,
Never missed and never will;
Always aims and shoots to kill
And the company pays his buffalo bill.

In 1883, when buffaloes were becoming scarce, Buffalo Bill turned his skills to entertainment. He set up a "Wild West Show" that featured bucking horses, sharp-shooters, and buffalo hunters. Over the years, millions of people in the United States and Europe rushed to see the traveling show.

In a buckskin jacket and broad-brimmed hat, Buffalo Bill staged a hunt for the audience. Sometimes he led a team of hunters; sometimes he performed alone. Buffaloes were chased into a large arena, where they milled about and then went to a water tank to drink. That's when Buffalo Bill charged in. Riding his trusty horse, he dashed among the buffaloes, firing blanks, not bullets.

The noise, smoke, and smell from the gunshots startled the animals. Snorting and wheeling about, they stampeded out of the arena with Buffalo Bill chasing them. And the audience went wild.

*Hollows made by rolling buffaloes
formed rain-filled watering holes
for settlers' cows and horses.*

a big problem for settlers. They just took the long way around until they met up with the trail on level ground again. They knew that these highways were the best routes to travel.

Along with the trails, buffaloes created many hollows by wallowing—rolling and rubbing their bulky bodies on the ground. That helped remove the hair they shed in spring and relieved the itching from insect bites. When they slammed their big humps against the ground, thrashing their legs about, they raised dust, which cleaned their fur and helped prevent more bites.

All this action created hollows that were often 2 feet (60 centimetres) deep and 10 feet (3 metres) across. When these hollows filled with rain, the settlers used them to water their livestock.

Picking the Bones

Long after the herds were gone, settlers used what was left of the buffalo. Families still warmed themselves with winter coats, overshoes, blankets, and sleigh robes that had once been woolly hides. Children still gathered dried buffalo dung to fuel fires where there were few trees. And settlers used the bones, horns, and hooves that lay strewn across the plains.

At trail crossings, for instance, a family might stop to read a sun-bleached buffalo skull, one of the "signboards of the plains." People often wrote messages on skulls, such as "Ruth: Went south to river. Harry."

To earn money during hard times, many settlers gathered buffalo bones to sell. Companies used the fresher bones to refine sugar and make bone china. They ground up older, drier bones into fertilizer. And they removed hair stuck to skulls to use as stuffing in pillows and mattresses.

Sometimes families gathered hooves for the glue market. They sold buffalo horns, too. Companies turned them into everything from buttons to combs.

Where buffalo parts weren't easy to find, some settlers burned tall prairie grass to expose bones and horns. Others

Horns to Handles

From little, black buttons come strong, hard horns. On both male and female buffaloes, horns grow thickest at the base, then narrow to sharp points. Horns of record-breaking size were found on a 25-year-old bull in the United States. The base of each was about 15 inches (38 centimetres) around. The spread between the curves of the horns was about 35 inches (89 centimetres); between horn tips, 27 inches (69 centimetres).

Companies that bought buffalo horns from settlers first removed the sticky material inside. They heated the horns, cutting and pressing them into shapes for knife handles, eyeglass frames, and ornaments. Then workers smoothed and polished these shapes to a hard shine. Some buyers never dreamed their knife handles had once grown on a buffalo head.

Pile upon pile of buffalo bones traveled by wagon and train to companies that used them to make such products as fertilizer.

traced old wheel tracks. If the tracks had been made by the wagons of buffalo skinners, they sometimes led to a pile of bones.

Wagonloads of these bones, horns, and hooves piled up beside railway tracks. There they waited to go to market. Some piles stood 12 feet (3.5 metres) tall and just as wide, and they stretched over half a mile (nearly a kilometre) long. Sad monuments to lost herds, they could be seen far across the prairie.

Toward the end of the nineteenth century, many of the remaining buffaloes lived on farms and ranches.

Remembering When

Memories of buffalo herds lived long after the herds themselves. Sitting around campfires or perched on fences, people loved to tell stories of buffalo times. Their most eager listeners were settlers who had seen—at most—a single buffalo here or there.

A storyteller might recall how calves just a few weeks old could hide among tall grass and bushes. At that age, too small to run when the herd stampeded, they "froze"—body still, eyes shut. One man had seen a cow return more than a day after she had run off with her herd. Sniffing the air for the scent of her calf, she had approached some bushes and grunted softly. The calf had run straight to her. To the man's surprise, it had been lying only 10 feet (3 metres) away, and he had not noticed it.

Many storytellers liked to talk about their narrow escapes from danger. They often told exciting tales, like the one about the hundreds of buffaloes that had gathered by a river. Two people standing just 600 feet (180 metres) away hadn't known the buffaloes were there. A thick tangle of bushes and trees had hidden the herd from view.

Suddenly, rifle fire had split the air and startled the buffaloes into stampeding. The sound of their hammering hooves had caused the two people to leap for safety. One had hung from a branch; the other had pressed against a narrow trunk. Smashing trees and flattening bushes, the frenzied animals had brushed against both people as they passed. Then, as suddenly as the herd had appeared, it was gone, and the people had stumbled off—shaken but unhurt.

Some of the most popular stories were about buffalo hunting, told by the hunters themselves. For them, there was no greater thrill than charging on horseback right into a speeding herd to take a shot. And with ears pressed back

Some hunters remembered a time when there were so many buffaloes that they cooked only the meat from the animal's hump.

Stories of buffalo hunts long past were stories of fast action and adventure.

and feet flying, their horses had seemed just as eager for the chase.

The hunters talked of many dangers. Their horses had stepped into gopher holes, plunging their riders head over heels to the ground. Buffaloes had suddenly turned their sharp horns against both horse and rider. But, to the hunters, these risks had only made the chase more stirring.

"Oh, how we loved it all," wrote James Schultz, who had hunted buffaloes in Montana, "the thunderous pounding and rattling of thousands of hooves; the sharp odor of the sage that they crushed; the accuracy of our shooting; the quick response of our trained horses to our directing hands. Always the run was over all too soon."

Memories of a First Hunt

*V*ictoria (Kildaw) Callihoo of the Alberta-Montana plains *remembered her first buffalo hunt well. She was 13 years old at the time, and she was accompanying her mother, a medicine woman. Setting the broken bones of injured hunters and giving medicine to the sick often kept her mother very busy.*

For that hunt in 1876, they joined about 100 other Metis families. Metis (say "may-tee") are people who are part European and part native North American. Together the families headed across the plains. Some traveled on horseback, but most rode squeaky wooden carts pulled by horses.

They hadn't traveled very far when they spotted a dark, moving mass: a huge herd of buffaloes. Riders with guns moved in quickly and made their kill. Then everyone helped bring the dead buffaloes to camp to prepare the meat and hides.

Victoria lived to be 104 years old. Thinking back on her first hunt, she wrote: "We, of those days, never could believe the buffaloes would ever be killed off, for there were thousands and thousands."

Chapter 5

Rugged Survivor

For North American buffaloes, the nineteenth century was almost their last. It began with people reporting herds that "blackened the plains as far as the eye could see" . . . herds so huge they measured 2 miles (3 kilometres) across and 25 miles (40 kilometres) deep.

In those days, about 60 million buffaloes roamed North America. Plains buffaloes lived from California to Pennsylvania, and from Mexico and Florida to British Columbia, Alberta, Saskatchewan, and Manitoba. Wood buffaloes lived in northern Canada—in British Columbia, Alberta, Saskatchewan, and the Northwest Territories.

But the numbers of buffaloes fell fast and far. By 1830, they had dropped to 40 million; just 60 years later there were only about 1,000 buffaloes left—including those in zoos.

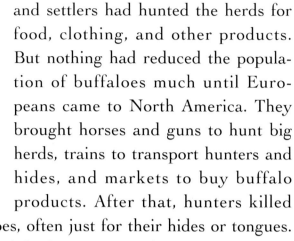

Native North American people and settlers had hunted the herds for food, clothing, and other products. But nothing had reduced the population of buffaloes much until Europeans came to North America. They brought horses and guns to hunt big herds, trains to transport hunters and hides, and markets to buy buffalo products. After that, hunters killed thousands of buffaloes, often just for their hides or tongues. During 1882—one of the biggest years for hunters—trains carried 200,000 hides out of Montana and North and South Dakota alone.

Going . . . Going . . .

Most people in the 1800s believed there would always be a lot of buffaloes, but a few worried that hunters were killing too many. As early as 1843, American naturalist John James Audubon warned, "Before many years the buffalo will have disappeared."

But it was 1894—and almost too late—before the United States government did anything effective to protect buffaloes. That year, it passed a law to fine or jail anyone who hunted the few buffaloes that lived in Yellowstone National Park, Wyoming. And several years later, it brought more buffaloes into the park to increase the small herd of about 20.

By the twentieth century, public respect for the buffalo was growing in the United States and Canada. In 1901, the animal appeared on the U.S. ten-dollar bill, nicknamed the "Buffalo-bill." In 1905, it took its place on the coat of arms of the Province of Manitoba, Canada.

By the end of the nineteenth century, hunters had reduced
huge herds of buffaloes to small, scattered groups.

In 1909, sightseers flocked to Buffalo National Park to see the first plains buffaloes shipped to Alberta from Montana.

Canada also passed a law in 1894 to protect both plains and wood buffaloes, but its plains buffaloes had almost completely disappeared. With three animals, the government began a small herd at Banff National Park, Alberta.

Interest in saving the buffalo began to grow in both countries. In 1907, the U.S. government created a buffalo range in Oklahoma, which later became the Wichita Mountains Wildlife Refuge. The government sent 15 buffaloes to start a herd there, and two years later sent another 34 to the new National Bison Range in Montana. Safe and well cared for, the herds thrived, and even more reserves and parks for buffaloes were created in the United States.

About the same time, Canada arranged to buy the largest remaining American herd from Michel Pablo, a Montana rancher. Paying $200 for each one, the government placed hundreds of buffaloes in Alberta—in Buffalo National Park and, for a short time, in Elk Island National Park.

Soon Canada's plains buffaloes began to multiply, but the number of wood buffaloes had fallen to about 300. So in 1922, the Canadian government created a park as big as Switzerland—Wood Buffalo National Park— to protect these wood buffaloes.

Safe!

By 1923, it seemed that both the United States and Canada had kept the buffalo from disappearing. In fact, the Yellowstone herd had grown so much that the park superintendent had buffaloes to give away to ranchers. Some people asked to have them as "furry pets" for their children, but buffaloes have never belonged in backyards.

At Canada's Buffalo National Park, the herd grew so fast that it

The Great Buffalo Roundup

*T*he longest, wildest buffalo roundup ever held in North America began in 1907. Over the next five years, rancher Michel Pablo and his hired hands struggled to move about 700 buffaloes from Montana to Alberta. Their goal was to sell the herd to Canada so the country could rebuild its population of plains buffaloes.

Using the best horses and some of the most experienced riders, Pablo drove buffaloes down rocky slopes, through deep ravines, and across rushing rivers. But the buffaloes had never been herded before. They took off again and again, stampeding madly across the plains. Sometimes they escaped by climbing cliffs so steep that horse and rider couldn't follow.

Frustrated, Pablo built a fence that stretched 26 miles (42 kilometres) from a buffalo pasture to some corrals. Riders drove the herd along the fence, then struggled to load the buffaloes from the corrals into a train. What a job! One buffalo burst right out of a boxcar, plunging through the wall as if it were tissue paper. And some of the animals escaped at the end of the train journey. Two old bulls broke out of a boxcar in central Alberta and walked all the way back to Montana— over 1200 miles (1900 kilometres).

soon ran out of space. Managers shipped more than 6,000 plains buffaloes to Wood Buffalo National Park, which turned out to be a terrible mistake. The newcomers brought in diseases. What's more, they mated with the wood buffaloes and produced calves that were part plains buffalo and part wood buffalo. Biologists feared that the wood buffalo would vanish.

But about 30 years later, wood buffaloes were spotted in a remote corner of Wood Buffalo National Park. A strip of land—mainly woods and bogs—had kept these animals from mixing much with the plains buffaloes. Using snow tractors to reach the rugged area, the biologists found about 200 of the animals—the closest living relatives of the original wood buffalo.

To make sure they wouldn't mix with other buffaloes, park officers moved some of the newfound herd to an area that was even more remote. They took others to Alberta's Elk Island National Park, where park managers used fences to keep wood and plains buffaloes apart.

Through the years, some parks, including Buffalo National Park, closed, but others opened to protect

Supercow?

If you crossed buffaloes with beef cattle, what would you get? Cattaloes? Beefaloes? Whatever you call them, they seem to survive winter's cold and summer's insects better than most cattle do. Like buffaloes, cattaloes also seem able to stand stronger winds, thrive on poorer grasses, and fight off more diseases.

As long ago as 1750, colonists in North America raised buffalo calves with cattle and bred cattaloes. Ever since, people have experimented with crossbreeds. They all wanted the same thing: a strong, hardy animal that produced meat that tasted like beef.

Although cattaloes were hardy, not all the males could reproduce, and many people still preferred the taste of cattle. Further, many ranchers began to feed their cattle in winter instead of putting them in open pastures where hardiness was more important. Interest in raising cattaloes fell.

Part buffalo and part cow, the cattalo was part of an experiment to combine the best of both.

more buffaloes. And ranchers set up private herds. Overall, the numbers of buffaloes in North America continued to grow.

Now and Forever

By 1994, about 200,000 buffaloes were living in North America. That's about 200 times more buffaloes than had lived there a century before. But with all the cities and farms we have today, there's no room for the millions of buffaloes that once roamed Canada and the United States. Still, buffaloes live in almost every province, territory, and state. Some even thrive in Hawaii, where buffaloes have never walked before.

Buffaloes need space to live as the wild animals they were born to be.

Many herds live on public land, such as parks; others live on private land, mainly ranches and zoos. One of the largest herds—nearly 6,000 buffaloes—lives on a big ranch in Montana. Like all ranchers, the owner raises the animals for meat and other products. But this owner makes sure the buffaloes range as freely as possible.

Managers of herds in large parks, such as Yellowstone National Park and Wood Buffalo National Park, also try to let buffaloes live as naturally as they can. That's usually best for the buffaloes—and best for the researchers who want to learn more about the ways of the herds.

But it's not easy to let buffaloes live as they have in the past. Although Yellowstone herds roam over 2 million acres (nearly a million hectares)

A buffalo coat kept this Royal Canadian Mounted Police (RCMP) officer warm in 1952.

of parkland, they sometimes leap over fences to munch the neighbors' grass. That upsets ranchers who want to keep their grassland for their cattle. They also worry that buffaloes might give their herds diseases.

Contact with people often changes the behavior of the buffalo. For instance, instead of struggling through deep snow in the winter, Yellowstone herds sometimes follow trails made by snowmobiles. The animals get used to the noise and smell of the snowmobiles— just as they get used to people and cars in the summer.

Biologists and nature lovers want to make sure that the buffalo survives, not just as a partly tame animal, but as the wild animal it was born to be. That means some herds must be allowed to live where only nature shapes their lives. One of the places where that's possible is in Canada's northern wilds. A herd of wood buffaloes introduced into the Yukon Territory, for instance, roams free, just like any other wildlife.

The struggle to save the buffalo in North America has been going on for more than a century. But it's worth the effort. If we can give our largest land animal a second chance, then we can hope to keep other wildlife from disappearing, too.

Hmmm, What's That?

*R*esearchers who study park buffaloes learn a lot about their behavior, including their curiosity. Like children, young buffaloes are natural explorers. They inspect objects that are new or different, such as lost combs or freshly painted fence posts. One researcher who always walked while he made notes about a herd sat down one day to write. In no time, several surprised buffaloes gathered around him.

Researchers have observed that buffalo curiosity is strongest when the animal feels safe and well fed. Then it can concentrate on exploring. With tail raised, it focuses its ears and eyes on the mystery object. It steps forward, slowly and cautiously. It sniffs a lot, putting its great sense of smell to use. Sometimes it also nudges the object with its nose or gives it a lick.

But curiosity dies fast if the object frightens the buffalo. Then the animal wheels around and runs off as fast as its hooves will take it.

Index

Photograph and Illustration Credits

Photographs

© Jim Brandenburg / First Light, vi

© Thomas Kitchin / First Light, 5

© Brian Milne / First Light, 6, 8

© Jeff Foott, 9, 10, 15, 38

© Head-Smashed-In Buffalo Jump, 20

© G. Petersen / First Light, 47

© Wayne Wegner / First Light, 52

Archival Photographs and Illustrations

Buffalo head, Saskatchewan Archives Board, University of Regina (R-A6716), all sidebars

Illustration appeared in *Historia General de las Indias*, Francisco Lopez de Gomara, 4

Hudson's Bay Company Archives, Provincial Archives of Manitoba

George Caitlin, *Buffalo Bull, Grazing* (N5214), 12

George Caitlin, *Buffalo Hunt, Surround* (N5221), 29

Currier & Ives, *The Buffalo Hunt* (N9518), 43

National Archives of Canada

Peter Rindisbacher, *Indian Hunter Pursuing the Buffalo in early spring* (C-114467), 26

Coke Smyth, *Buffalo Hunting* (C-001030), 32

Illustration appeared in *A Pictorial Archive from Nineteenth Century Sources*, 14

Illustration appeared in *Canadian Illustrated News* (1875), 17

Illustration appeared in *Century Magazine*, 18

Western Canada Pictorial Index, A.J. Miller, *Buffalo Jump* (1334-39857), 25

Harper's Weekly

(August 2, 1884) buffalo and train, 30

(March 10, 1877) S.E. Waller, 42

Buffalo Bill advertising booklet published in 1898 by Courier Co., Buffalo N.Y., 36

Glenbow Archives, Calgary, Alberta (NA 250-15), 40, (NA 4118-9), 41, (NA 1792-3), 48, (NA 424-7), 51

Manitoba coat of arms, Minister of Culture, Heritage and Citizenship for Manitoba, 46

Royal Canadian Mounted Police Photo Library (1283-1), 53

About the Author

Born and raised in Lethbridge, Alberta, Diane Swanson specializes in nature writing for children. She is the author of *The Day of the Twelve-Story Wave*, *Sky Dancers*, *Coyotes in the Crosswalk*, *Why Seals Blow Their Noses*, *A Toothy Tongue and One Long Foot*, and *Squirts and Snails and Skinny Green Tails*. In 1995, she received the Orbis Pictus Award for outstanding nonfiction for children from the National Council of Teachers of English for her book, *Safari Beneath the Sea*. Through frequent visits to libraries and schools, Diane shares her enthusiasm for nature with hundreds of children each year. She lives in Victoria, British Columbia.